Read-About® Science

Tiny Life on the Ground

By Mary Dodson Wade

Consultants

Reading Adviser
Nanci Vargus, EdD
Assistant Professor of Literacy
University of Indianapolis
Indianapolis, Indiana

Subject Adviser
Howard A. Shuman, PhD
Department of Microbiology
Columbia University Medical Center
New York, New York

Children's Press®
A Division of Scholastic Inc.
New York   Toronto   London   Auckland   Sydney
Mexico City   New Delhi   Hong Kong
Danbury, Connecticut

Designer: Herman Adler Design
Photo Researcher: Caroline Anderson
The photo on the cover shows soil bacteria.

Library of Congress Cataloging-in-Publication Data

Wade, Mary Dodson.
  Tiny life on the ground / by Mary Dodson Wade.
      p. cm. — (Rookie read-about science)
  Includes index.
  ISBN 0-516-25298-4 (lib. bdg.)   0-516-25479-0 (pbk.)
  1. Soil microbiology—Juvenile literature. I. Title. II. Series.
  QR111.W13 2005
  579'.1757—dc22
                                     2005004724

CHILDREN'S PRESS, and ROOKIE READ-ABOUT®,
and associated logos are trademarks and/or registered trademarks
of Scholastic Library Publishing. SCHOLASTIC and associated logos
are trademarks and/or registered trademarks of Scholastic Inc.

1 2 3 4 5 6 7 8 9 10 R 14 13 12 11 10 09 08 07 06 05

These apple trees are full of apples. What happens when the apples fall to the ground?

Animals eat the apples.
Some animals you can see,
such as a squirrel.

Every day plants, insects,
and other animals die.
They fall to the ground,
just like the apples. Does
something eat them, too?

Yes! They get eaten by tiny living things.

These tiny living things are bacteria (bak-TIHR-ee-uh) and fungus.

Bacteria are not animals. They are not plants.

Plants and animals are made up of millions of parts, called cells (SELLS).

Bacteria are another kind of life. Bacteria only have one cell.

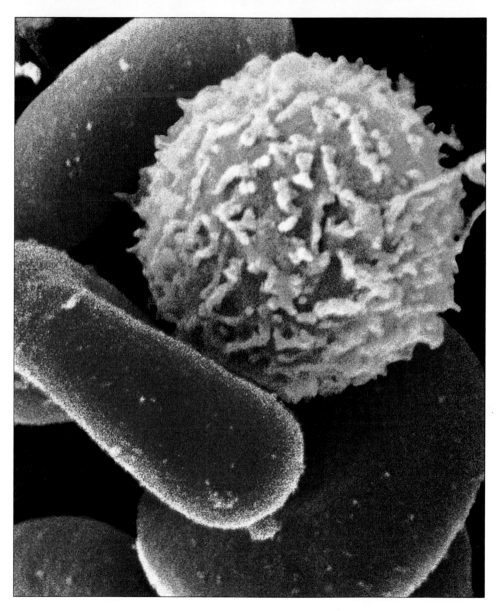

Bacteria are very small. They are so small that you can't see them.

A spoonful of dirt has about 1 billion bacteria in it.

Bacteria eat dead plants, fruit, leaves, and animals. Bacteria help the dead plants and animals turn into soil.

13

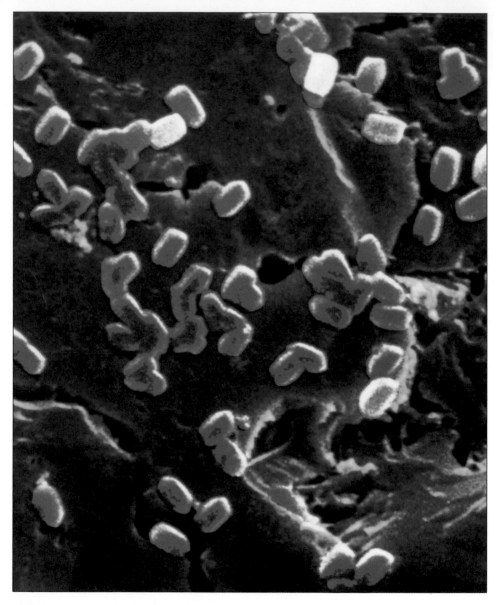

14

Bacteria are among the oldest living things on Earth. Bacteria have been found in fossils.

Some fossils are more than 3 million years old.

Some bacteria live in places too hot or too cold for people to live.

This hot spring has bacteria in it. That's what causes the color.

17

18

Bacteria help clean up pollution. Pollution can make people sick and kill plants and animals.

This is an oil spill. An oil spill is a kind of pollution. Bacteria can help clean this up.

Fungus is another kind of tiny life. Some fungi you can see, but some fungi are tiny.

A spoonful of soil may have 120,000 tiny fungi in it.

22

Some tiny fungi live on the ground. They eat dead plants and animals.

Some fungi help insects.

Cutter ants cut leaves to eat. The ants need help to eat the leaves.

The ants give the leaves to the fungus. The fungus eats the leaves. It turns the leaves into food the ants can eat.

The next time you walk
in the woods, look at
the ground.

Tiny living things are hard
at work, even if you can't
see them.

Words You Know

apples

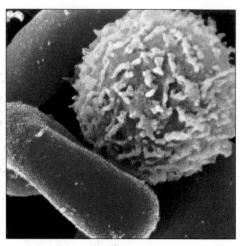

cells

cutter ant

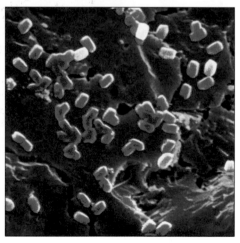

fossil

fungus

hot spring

oil spill

soil

Index

About the Author

Mary Dodson Wade has published more than forty books, including biographies as well as science books. She worked for many years as an elementary-school librarian, a job that revealed interesting topics for children. Ms. Wade and her husband, Harold, live in Houston, Texas. They travel frequently to visit their daughter in Boston, and their son and granddaughter, Melia, in Honolulu.

Photo Credits

Photographs ©: 2005: Corbis Images: 13 (Andrew Brown/Ecoscene), 18, 31 bottom left (Natalie Fobes), 25, 30 bottom left (Michael & Patricia Fogden), 3, 30 top left (Patrick Johns), 17, 31 top right (Wolfgang Kaehler), 5 (George McCarthy), 6 (Peter Reynolds/Frank Lane Picture Agency); Nance S. Trueworthy: 10, 31 bottom right; Peter Arnold Inc.: 22 (S. J. Krasemann), cover (David Scharf); Photo Researchers, NY/Gregory G. Dimijian: 26; PhotoEdit/David Young-Wolff: 29; Phototake/Frances Westall/Eurelios: 14, 30 bottom right; Stone/Getty Images/Yorgos Nikas: 9, 30 top right; TRIP Photo Library/C. Toms: 21, 31 top left.